MOVIE VOCAL SELECTIONS

THE PRODUCERS

MUSIC AND LYRICS BY
MEL BROOKS

ISBN 1-4234-0989-2

HAL•LEONARD®
CORPORATION
7777 W. BLUEMOUND RD. P.O. BOX 13819 MILWAUKEE, WI 53213

In Australia Contact:
Hal Leonard Australia Pty. Ltd.
4 Lentara Court
Cheltenham, Victoria, 3192 Australia
Email: ausadmin@halleonard.com

Visit Hal Leonard Online at
www.halleonard.com

CONTENTS

OPENING NIGHT

Music and Lyrics by
MEL BROOKS

WE CAN DO IT

Music and Lyrics by
MEL BROOKS

18

19

I WANNA BE A PRODUCER

Music and Lyrics by
MEL BROOKS

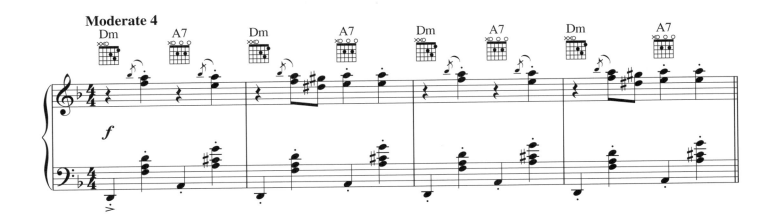

LEO & ACCOUNTANTS:

Un - hap - py, un - hap - py, ver - y un - hap - py,

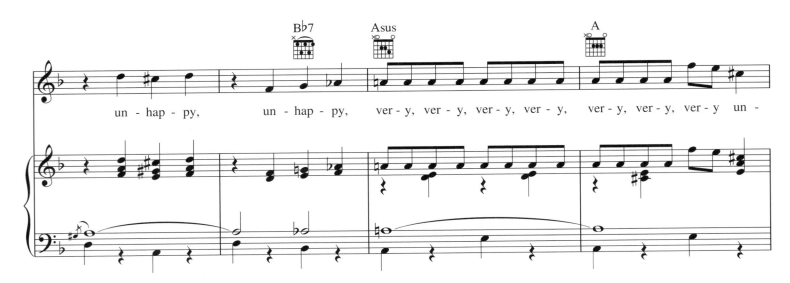

un - hap - py, un - hap - py, ver - y, ver - y, ver - y, ver - y, ver - y, ver - y, ver - y un -

SOLO ACCOUNTANT:

hap - py. Oh, I deb - its all de morn - in' and I

rit. *colla voce*

ACCOUNTANTS:

cred - its all de eve - nin' un - til dem ledg - ers be right. Un -

con moto

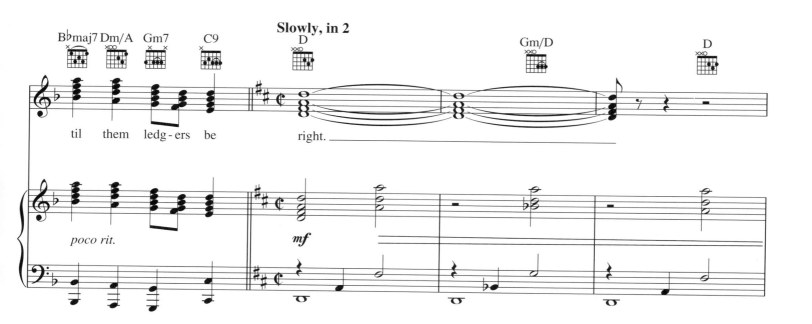

Slowly, in 2

til them ledg - ers be right. _____

poco rit. *mf*

LEO:
I spend my life ac - count - ing with fig - ures and

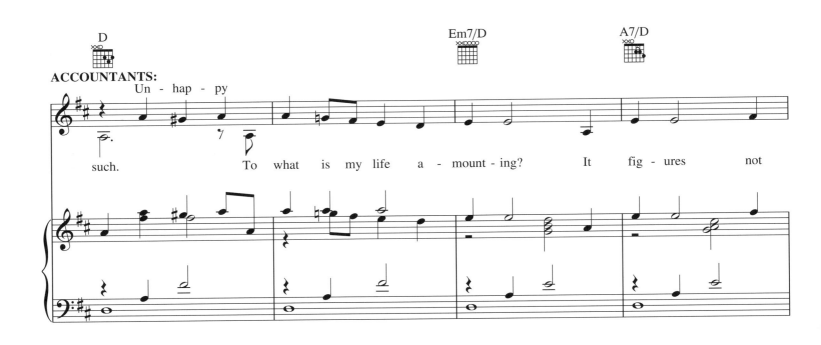

ACCOUNTANTS:
Un - hap - py
such. To what is my life a - mount - ing? It fig - ures not

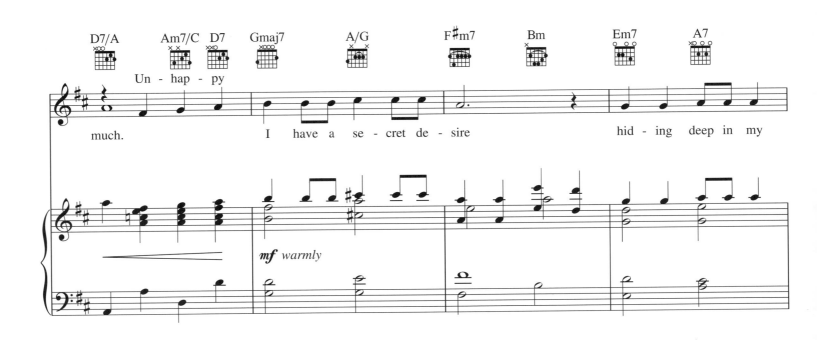

Un - hap - py
much. I have a se - cret de - sire hid - ing deep in my

mf warmly

soul. It sets my heart a-fire ____ to see me in this

role. ____

Softshoe, in 4

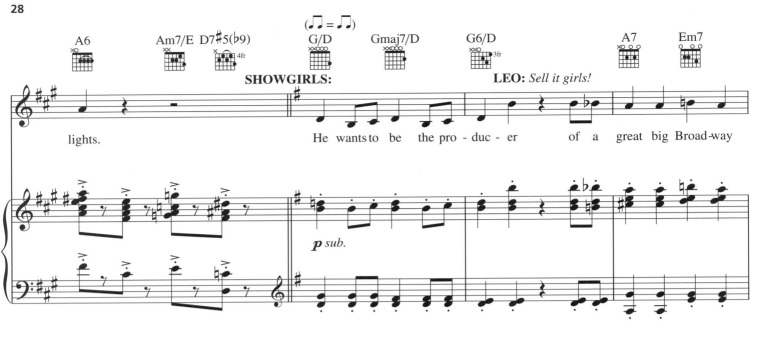

SHOWGIRLS:

LEO: *Sell it girls!*

lights.

He wants to be the pro-duc-er of a great big Broad-way

p sub.

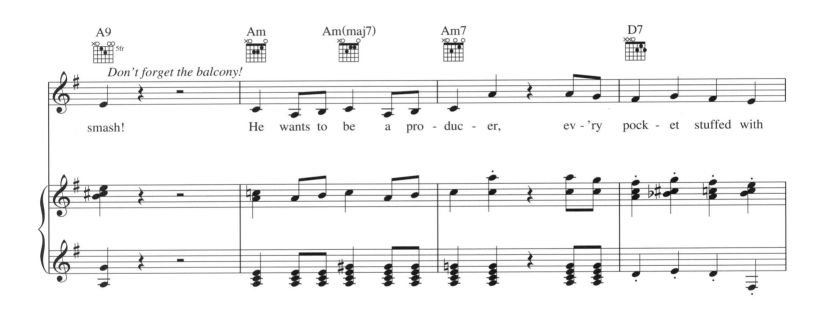

Don't forget the balcony!

smash!

He wants to be a pro-duc-er, ev-'ry pock-et stuffed with

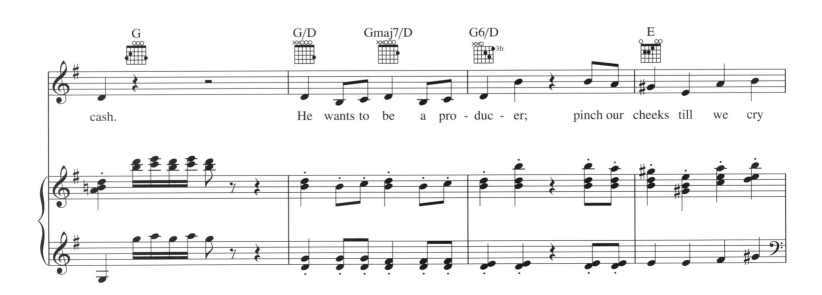

cash.

He wants to be a pro-duc-er; pinch our cheeks till we cry

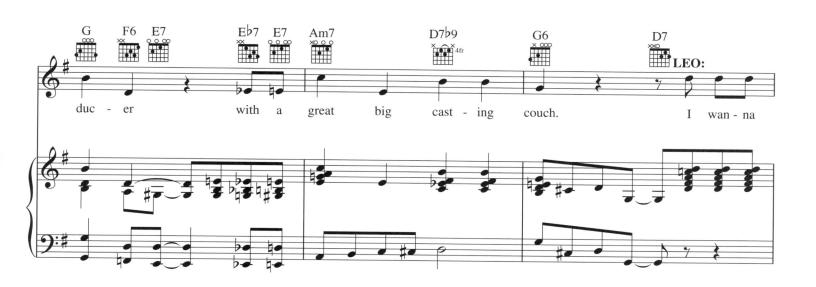

DER GUTEN TAG HOP-CLOP

Music and Lyrics by
MEL BROOKS

KEEP IT GAY

Music and Lyrics by
MEL BROOKS

Moderate Waltz

ROGER:

(Spoken:) Exactly! No mat-ter what you do on the stage keep it

light, keep it bright, keep it gay. Wheth-er it's mur -

der, may-hem or rage, don't com-plain, it's a pain, keep it

gay. _____ Peo - ple want

40

WHEN YOU GOT IT, FLAUNT IT

Music and Lyrics by
MEL BROOKS

43

Broad Swing

ALONG CAME BIALY

Music and Lyrics by
MEL BROOKS

al - y! They were joy - less, __ they were boy - less, __ then a -

long came Bi - al - y! They're my an - gels, __ I'm their

dev - il, __ and I keep those em - bers a - glow. __ When I woo 'em, __ I can't

lose 'em, __ 'cause I cast my spell 'n' they start yell - in' fi - re down be - low! They were

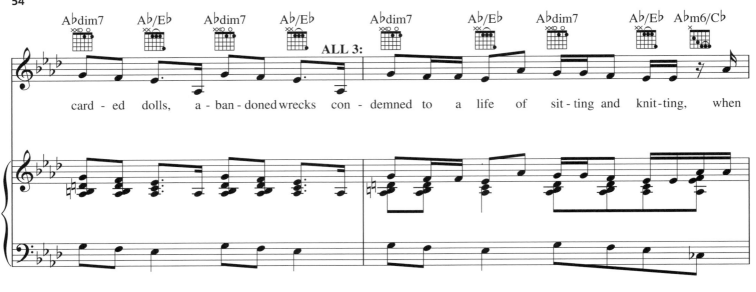

card - ed dolls, a - ban - doned wrecks con - demned to a life of sit - ting and knit - ting, when

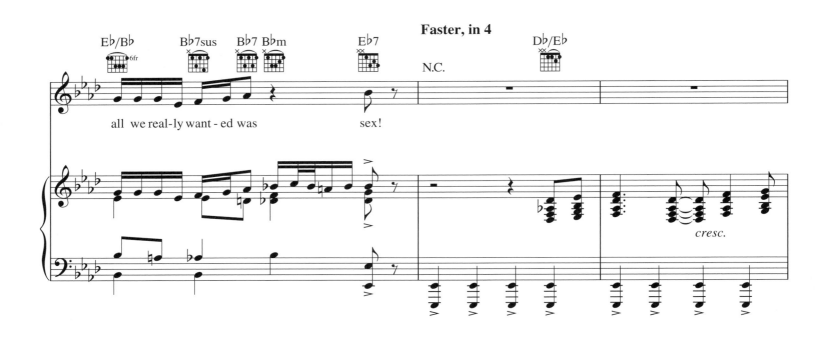

all we real-ly want - ed was sex!

We were

THAT FACE

Music and Lyrics by
MEL BROOKS

LEO: The urge to merge can rob us of our sens-es. The need to breed can make a man a drone. We must be on a-lert with our de-

fens - es   for ev - 'ry skirt will test tes - tos - ter - one.   So

know - ing this, I sev - ered all con - nec - tion   with an - y crea - ture sport - ing silk or

più mosso

lace.   I was firm - ly head - ed in the right di - rec - tion   when

Slowly

sud - den - ly I stum - bled on that face.   That

HABEN SIE GEHÖRT DAS DEUTSCHE BAND?

(Have You Ever Heard the German Band?)

Music and Lyrics by
MEL BROOKS

Bright March, in 2

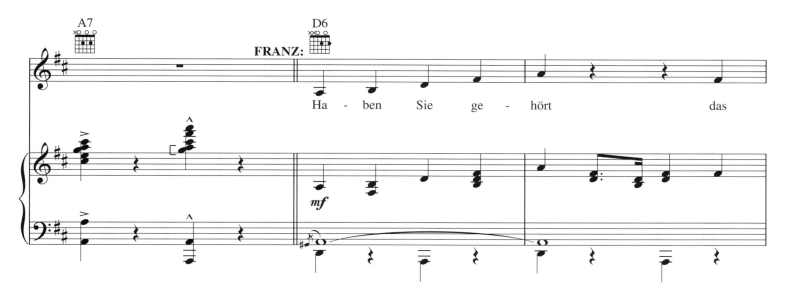

Haben Sie ge-hört das

Deut-sche band? Mit a bang, mit a

64

stu - pid und they're rot - ten!   It don't mean a

thing   if   it   ain't   got that Schwei - gen Rei - gen schö - nen Schüt - zen

Schmüt - zen Sau - er - bra - ten. *Key change!* Ve're   say - in'

Pull back

Ha - ben Sie ge - hört   das   Deut - sche   band? ___

YOU NEVER SAY GOOD LUCK
ON OPENING NIGHT

Music and Lyrics by
MEL BROOKS

70

71

nev - er say good luck on op-'ning night. That's the rule, I'm no

LEO: *Break a leg?*
ROGER, CARMEN & FRANZ: *Yes, break a leg!*

ROGER, CARMEN & FRANZ:

fool. What do I say, I beg? What you say is "break a leg!"

poco rit.   *colla voce*   *fp*

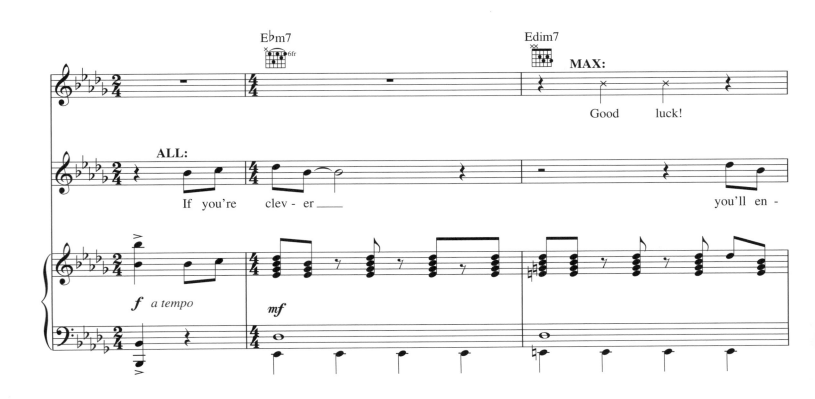

MAX:

Good luck!

ALL:

If you're clev - er ___ you'll en -

f a tempo   *mf*

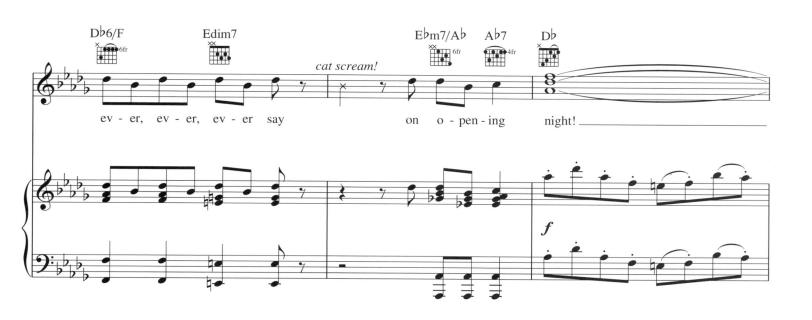

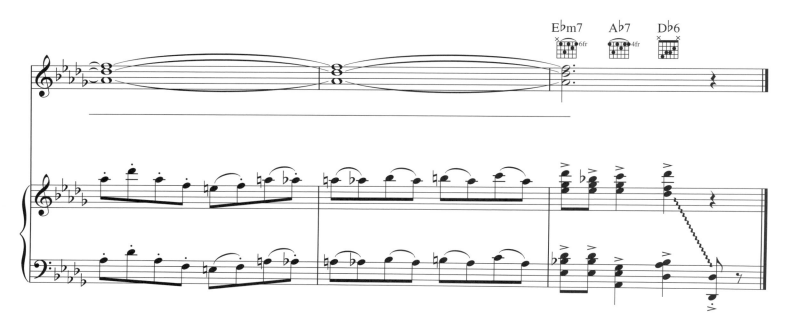

SPRINGTIME FOR HITLER

Music and Lyrics by
MEL BROOKS

Fast 2

CHORUS:

Ger-ma-ny was hav-ing trou-ble, what a sad, sad sto-ry,

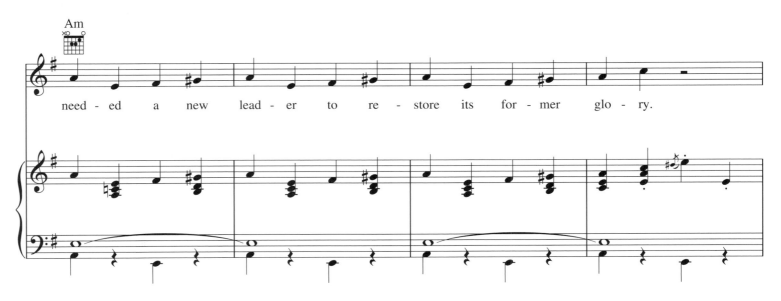

need-ed a new lead-er to re-store its for-mer glo-ry.

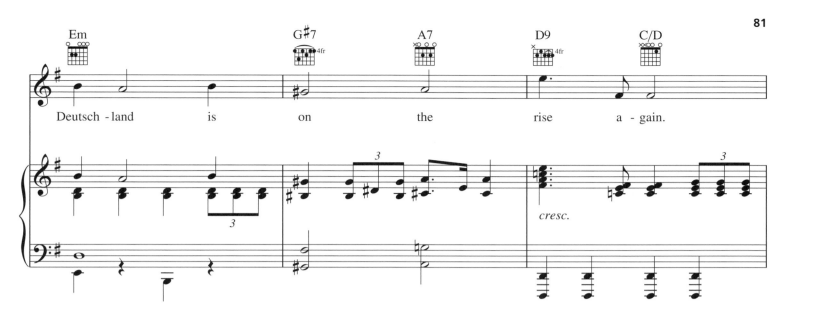

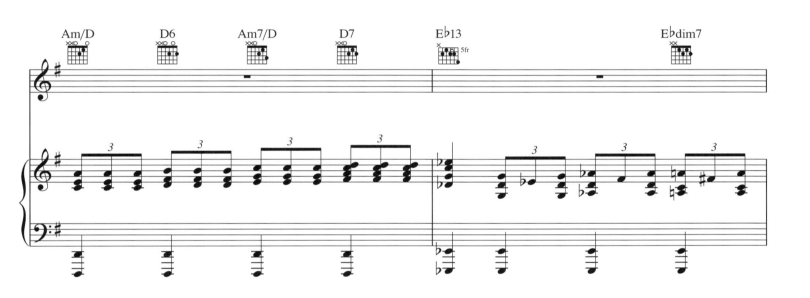

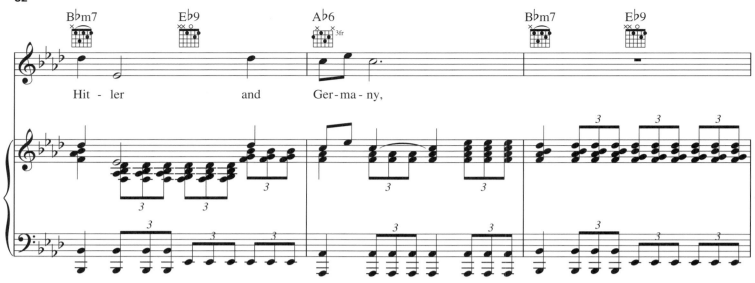

Hit - ler and Ger - ma - ny,

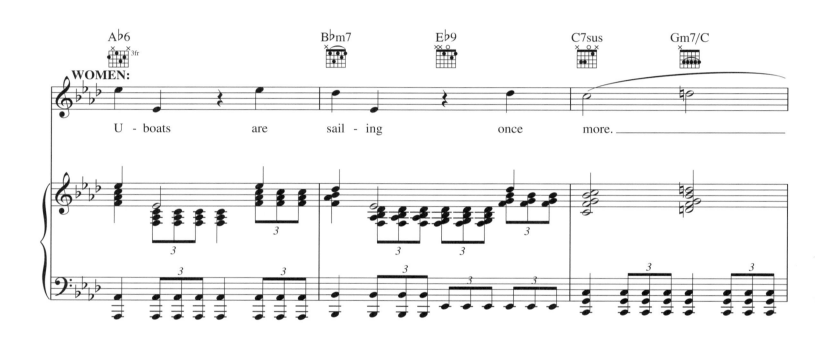

WOMEN:

U - boats are sail - ing once more. _____

_____ Spring - time for Hit - ler and Ger - ma - ny

84

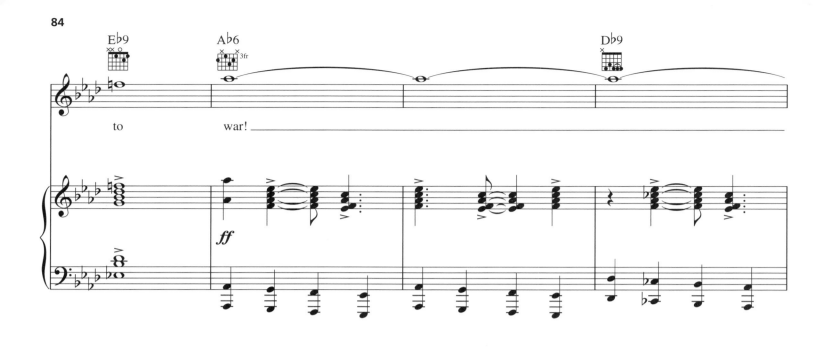

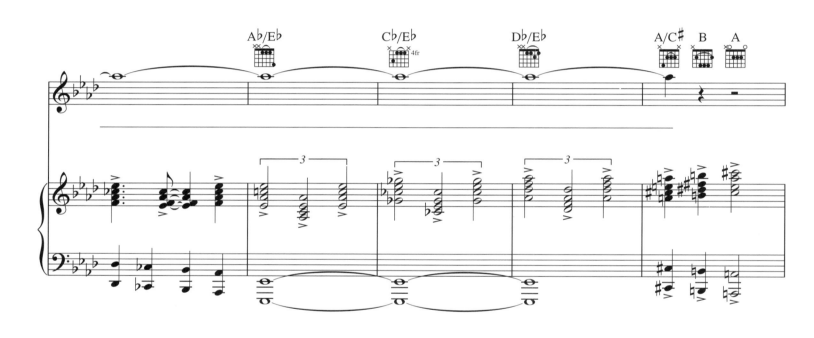

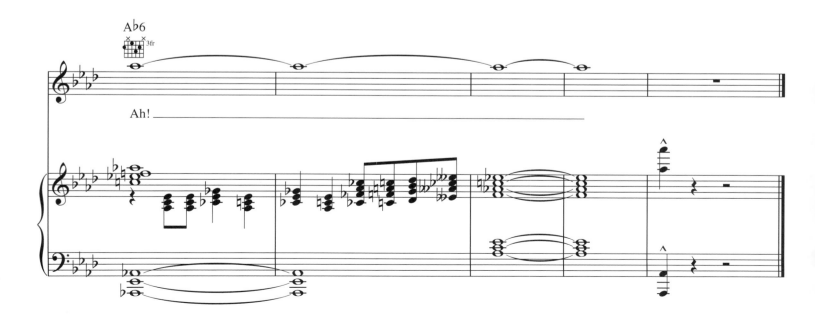

HEIL MYSELF

Music and Lyrics by
MEL BROOKS

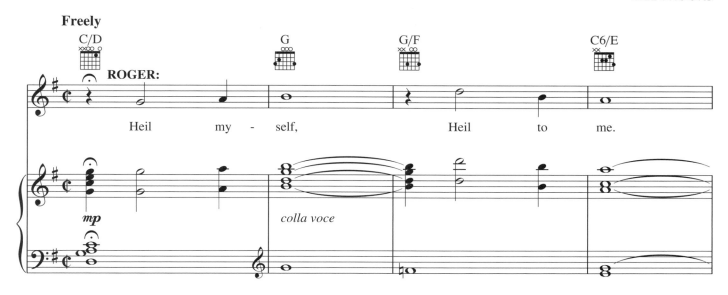

*Until noted, the downstemmed male notes sound as written. (Normally, these notes would appear an octave higher.)

88

*Normal male voice notation.

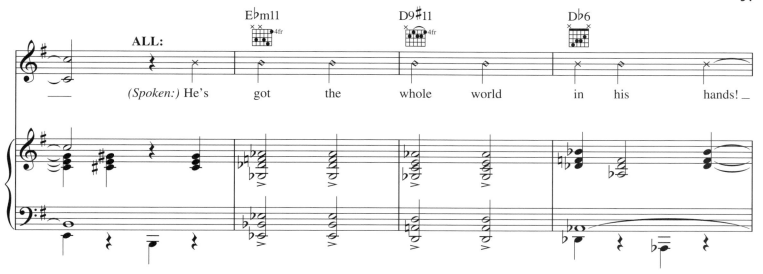

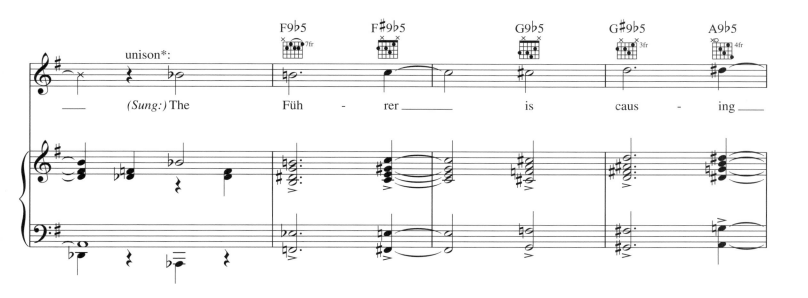

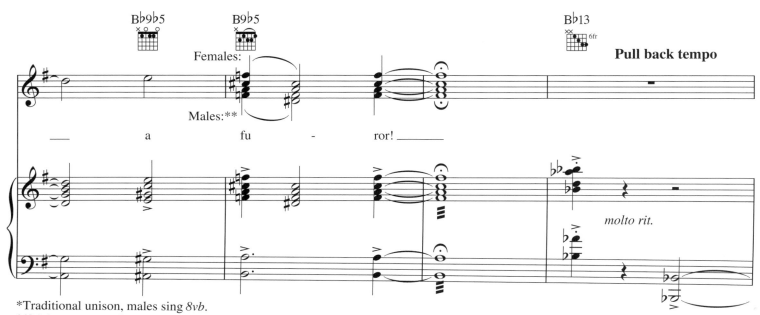

*Traditional unison, males sing *8vb.*
**Male notes as written. (Normally would appear an octave higher.)

*Male notes as written. (Normally would appear an octave higher.)

93

YOU'LL FIND YOUR HAPPINESS IN RIO

Music and Lyrics by
MEL BROOKS

Hot Latin Beguine-ish

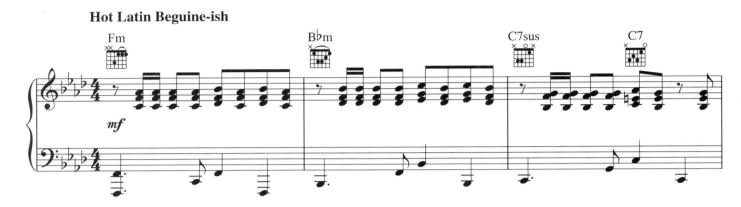

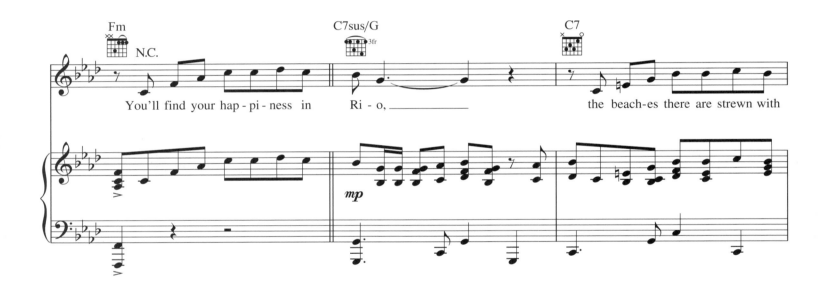

You'll find your hap-pi-ness in Ri - o, _____ the beach-es there are strewn with

pearls. The trop-ic breez-es al-ways blow there, _____

vine. _____ Let's all es-cape to Ri - o, _____

vine. _____ Let's all es-cape to

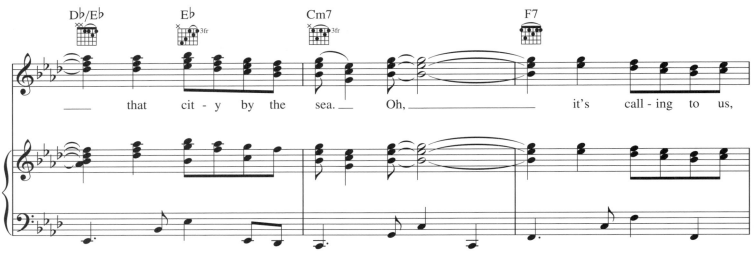

_____ that cit - y by the sea. ___ Oh, _____ it's call-ing to us,

Le - o! ___ Let's make it yours and mine!

BETRAYED

Music and Lyrics by
MEL BROOKS

Sam-son and De-li-lah, your love be-gan to fade. I'm cry-ing in the hoose-gow, you're in

Ri-o get-ting laid! Be-trayed! _____ Let's face it, I'm be-

trayed! Boy, _____

have I been tak-en.

MAX: *I'm drowning! I'm drowning here! I'm going down for the last time! I see my whole life flashing before my eyes!*

(Spoken above the "bucolic" interlude)
MAX: *I see a weathered old farmhouse, and a white picket fence. I'm running through fields of alfalfa with my collie, Rex.*
And I see my mother, standing on the back porch, in a worn but clean gingham gown, and I hear her calling out to me,
"Alvin! Alvin! Don't forget your chores. The wood needs a cordin' and the cows need a milkin'. Alvin, Alvin..."

'TIL HIM

Music and Lyrics by
MEL BROOKS

112

PRISONERS OF LOVE
(Leo & Max)

Music and Lyrics by
MEL BROOKS

Fast Show-Biz 2

CONVICT #1:

Got - ta sing - sing!

CONVICT #2:

Got - ta sing - sing!

MAX: *OK boys, break's over.*
Let's take it from the top.

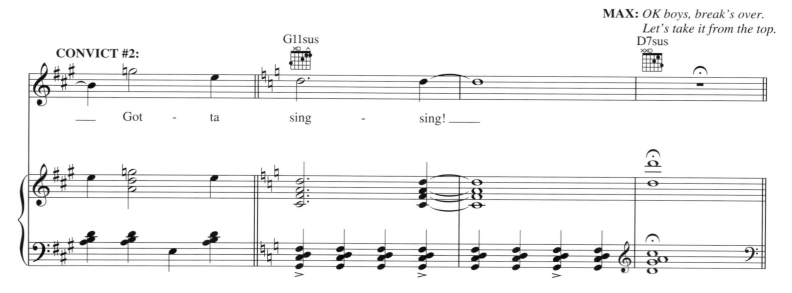

THERE'S NOTHING LIKE A SHOW ON BROADWAY

Music and Lyrics by
MEL BROOKS

Somewhat freely, not too slow

The o-ver-ture is o-ver, the cur-tain starts to rise. You're sud-den-ly in clo-ver, you can't be-lieve your eyes. You're sit-ting on the aisle, you break in-to a smile. Why this mag-ic feel-ing? And then you re-al-ize

126

THE HOP-CLOP GOES ON

Music and Lyrics by
MEL BROOKS

135

GOODBYE!

Music and Lyrics by
MEL BROOKS

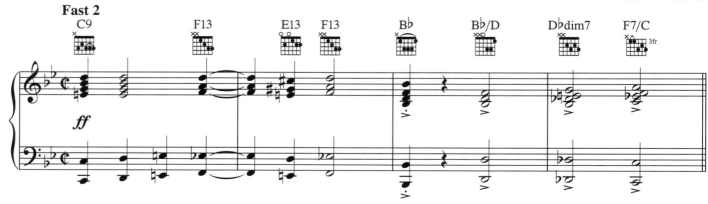

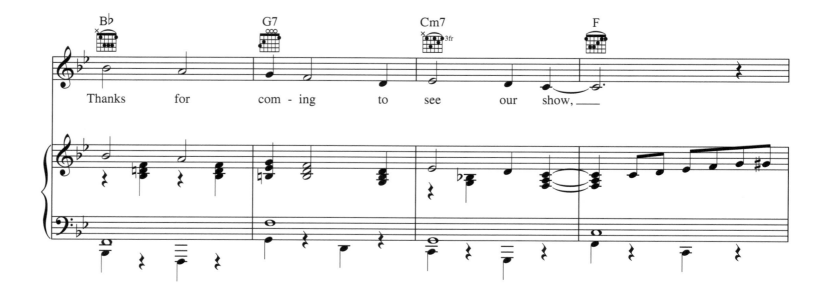

Thanks for com-ing to see our show, ____

sad to tell you we got to go. ____

THE KING OF BROADWAY

Music and Lyrics by
MEL BROOKS

I used to be the king, the king of old Broad-way. The best of ev-'ry-thing was mine to have each day. I al-ways had the big-gest hits, the